At Home on Upper Beaver Creek

Christine M. Kendall

AT HOME ON UPPER BEAVER CREEK

For Jack, who made moving to Beaver Creek happen.
Thank you for this adventure and all the joy it brings.

CONTENTS

PART 3:

SUMMER

FOREWORD

The compilation of the poems in *At Home on Upper Beaver Creek* grew from hearing that Jennifer Molesworth planned to curate a Confluence Gallery exhibit in Twisp featuring the artists of Upper and Lower Beaver Creek Roads. I began pulling together poetry I had written inspired by my experiences of living with Jack on our property in the Methow Valley on Upper Beaver Creek. While we sheltered in place during the Covid-19 pandemic, I regularly walked our dog, Gus, around our upper and lower fields, and felt a deeper connection to the land, its wildlife, and seasons, which inspired many new poems in this volume.

I know in the scheme of things, we are newcomers to this environment, and only guests on land we share with other creatures whose home it is as well. We co-exist and appreciate these neighbors. Recently, one evening at dusk, a moose walked through our property, and we had the thrill of seeing her. It's almost impossible to put into words the joyous rush of such a sighting, that for a few minutes, this visitor gifted us with her rare presence as she ambled across the alfalfa field, and then lithely jumped the fence between our field and our neighbors. *At Home on Upper Beaver Creek* is about small moments like this; they pass by, but bring such delight into our lives, and make Jack and me glad we chose to live on Upper Beaver Creek.

—Christine M. Kendall

WINTER

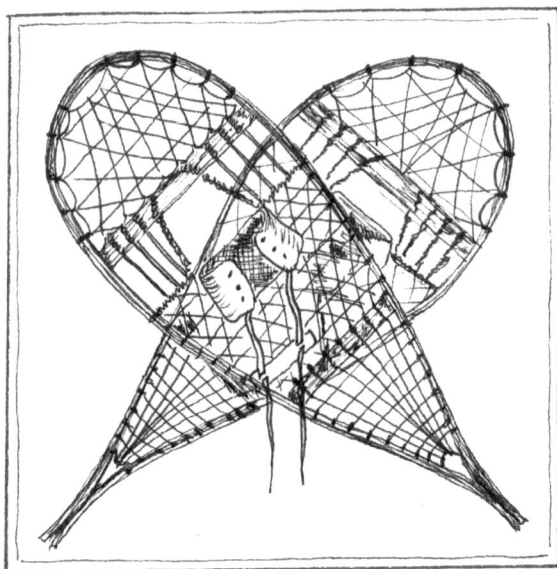

The Call

The sharp scree of a Red-tailed Hawk
fills my ears, whistles through sky.
I am called to pause and consider this
high pitched sound, this scree trailing off
to a whisper, remnant of it an earworm.

It's a birdcall that begs attention be paid,
like bells ringing the Angelus for prayers,
a singing bowl or gong for meditation.
It awakens me—mind and body together,
in the Methow, these sounds, these pauses,
become wayfinders to inner peace.

Softly, silently, snow fell in the night,
whitened the ground, left round clumps
in bushes, lodged in crotches of trees,
changed surroundings from spring's
promise with leaves of crocus spiking up
to a glistening carpet signaling a delay.

An almost blank canvas only a painterly eye
could find color in: topaz haystacks, subtle
hues of deciduous trees, cinnamon in Ponderosa
pine bark, red or blue spots of shriveled berries,
snow— as chameleon—changes to shades
of grey, chilling blues, pinks, purple, and orange.

The snow-bright light is not unwelcome to us
coming as it does before the dreaded mud season
when frozen earth thaws and becomes gooey,
caking up on boots and car tires and wheelwells.
There are six seasons in the Methow, including
mud and fire, and no perfect calendar for them.

DIRT

Snow will soon cover the soil,
that industrious substance
most of us know so little about,
where diversity is greater than we
can calculate, where exchanges make
our own sense of commerce—the sacrosanct
stock market—mom and pop enterprises.

Microbes, infinitesimally small, do more
than anything we can imagine. Come spring,
in our gardens, we can grasp a clump of dirt
in one hand, and hold an entire world.

WAKE UP

Bam, bam! Two birds hit my bedroom window,
first, a quail, followed by a peregrine falcon.
The quail dropped like a stone while the falcon
fell a few feet from it, landing on his back, his feet
pedaled sky, pedaled for all his might as if to grab
an updraft to lift him and to let him escape
gravity, or death; watching him I held my breath
only to see him roll to his side, one leg,
and one wing bent, disarranged. Yet, somehow
he swam his way atop a snowdrift and sat,
then to my surprise after flapping hops he flew
in awkward flight, landed on a limb of a tree,
waggled his tail and body as if testing all systems
one-by-one, like any good pilot doing a preflight
check, and then, at last, he flew away with grace.

Gus

goes into my closet, points out snow pants
with his nose, in suggestion I suit up and take
him outside, and so I do. I get my snowshoes
on as he impatiently waits for me to begin
our trek, creating pathways, a circuit to follow,
places to pause to take in the dazzle.

The white, cold world of snow is a joy to him,
he sniffs to investigate critters beneath it, then
runs, as if through waves, in leaps and bounds.
All through winter, he's exceptionally clean,
we miss snow season for that reason alone.

Coming here at eight weeks old in February,
he marched to the top of a pile of snow taller
then I am, marked his presence here, and his
complete acceptance of this climate, so different
from the warm whelping box he was raised in.

As snow melted away, he found patches to play in,
like an old friend he was glad to see. His new friend
will be shade to seek out spring, summer, and fall.
Together we'll await the first flakes of snow.

MALLARDS ALONG BEAVER CREEK

A snowy day, a milky sky met ground, my world
a gessoed canvas. Then, a mallard flew by, a blast
of color, emerald green head magnificent, a patch
of teal blue like a badge; drakes wear brilliant colors.

As children, finding our dad's duck call was a joyous
discovery; we loved being ducks, quacking around
the house; we had no idea of sounds real ducks made,
or the quiet whistle of their wing beats.

In winter, mallards angle in and out of our neighbor's field,
feasting upon corn he feeds his cattle; they pattern sky,
providing interest to our winter days. The one who came
so close we were eye-to-eye, still vivid in my mind.

WINTER'S DAY PHENOMENA

Overnight, wet slushy snow
froze on our metal roof.
When the sun rose
and warmed the world,
large translucent sheets
slipped off, one-by-one,
catching light,
lustrous
in their descents.

They shattered
on banked snow;
shards overlapped,
except two, lodged intact
like icy tombstones
without inscriptions.

WHAT'S LEFT

Wring out this body of mine,
and what's left but a pile
of bones, flesh, sinew, ligament.

The latter will rot away, but those
bones could be strung together
to clack in the wind, let them.

Let the moisture of me seep
into the earth, filtering down,
tapped someday to sustain

new life in another form,
germination of a seed to send it
up and up striving for light.

METHOW WEATHER REPORT

Today, ice thin as onion skin
formed between ribs on metal
rooftops, melted, as the day
warmed, slid slowly to eaves,
slipped off in small rectangles—

translucent postcards of capricious
weather fluttered down—
Jack delivered one to me
on the palm of his hand.

DEER

wander at night
in snow, leaving tracks
like stitches on a quilt.
I go out in daylight
wearing snowshoes,
overlap footprints,
and make a trail.
The next day I notice
deer use my trodden path
—a freeway of sorts—
to expedite
roving in darkness.

I feel like a road builder,
my oval steps a giant's
alongside dainty tracks;
a story of deer travel
is written in their calligraphy
beneath star-dazzled
skies, while owls
call out claims
of territory.

Inside our house
we sleep a sound
winter night's sleep
while creatures
nocturnal are free
from our intrusion.
Some mornings, I see
curved depressions
in snow where deer
have slept, as well.

SNOWPLOW SIDEWALKS

A road grader
leveled banks of snow
along our country road,
and it now appears
we have sidewalks,
a surprising sight
on this road
without a centerline
or fog lines—how curbed
and citified it looks—
changed into something
I wouldn't want it to be.

PINE TREES—TWO VIEWS

—With thanks to e.e. cummings

Above Beaver Creek
a snowy hillside against
whitened sky portrays
pine trees on a ridgeline
like folded paper cutouts
snipped out of fog—
then spread wide—as if God
played with scissors.

A second look shifts
pine trees to the foreground,
snow and fog recede, the sweet
surprise of the unexpected vanishes—
a trick of light and perception
or "now the eyes of my eyes are opened."

Life Cycles in the Methow

Born in winter, Black Angus calves
find their legs then frolic with others;
a band of youth discovering their kind
and their world—doting mothers—snow
caping their backs—keep watch.

An array of avian scavengers waits patiently:
eagles, hawks, ravens, and magpies roost
in cottonwoods by the creek overlooking
the birthing field, watching for afterbirth
to feast upon; they'll swoop down to ingest
placentas—a satisfying meal, nutrient-rich—
it repays their diligence, fuels their bodies.

On Upper Beaver Creek long before signs
of spring—it's an almost monochromatic world—
a few dashes of bright color: red, blue, yellow,
green and orange in idle farm machinery,
except for a nearby rancher's New Holland
tractor bearing load after load of hay to his herd.

New life is born, life cycles sustained—
cows fertilize fields their feed will grow in,
satiate large birds about to settle into nests—
and we who witness this are not as separate
from it as it may seem sheltered in our houses
or automobiles—binoculars or spotting scopes
to our eyes.

THE PRIZE

The dog brought home a coyote
skull, a bone to him,
a scent, a treasure, not kith
and kin. Stripped clean,
there's no connection
to howls that prick up
his ears after dark.

No connection to marks
left—intoxicants to sniff—
he knows coyotes by whiffs
on a breeze, he's seen them
in the distance tracking across
fields. Once, a coyote chased
him, my high-pitched screams
diverting it.

We kept the skull. Hollow
sockets once held watchful eyes,
the cranium a brain, and
ears to hear other packs howl
on hillsides; tonight progeny
will watch a full moon rise.

SPRING

AVIAN SYMPHONY

Ravens use all their voices today:
squawks, croaks, ratchey rasps,
the familiar *tock-tock-tocks*, even
mewling puppy sounds.

Such a repertoire and broadcast
of intentions or desires: calling
for a mate, claiming territory,
or advertising a smorgasbord?

My human brain tries to make sense
of the symphony as other players join in:
red-winged blackbird, California quail,
finches, chickadees, Eurasian collared doves,
and more. Before dawn the great conductor
taps his baton, and it all begins.

A Fascination of Ravens

From the top of our knoll, I look down to see
Beaver Creek filled with sky, looking up, the sky
is filled with ravens, wind is their amusement:
they undulate as if on a roller coaster, then glide,
and spiral until a gust slides them all to the south,
back they come calling one another as they circle
five pine trees on our little hill.

I stand atop the hill; they skim just above my head.
First their calls click like little gears whir and move
them, then yelps like children yelling, "Wait up, wait up."
A new game begins with pinecones grasped, dropped,
caught, and passed to another with dexterity and grace.

This has been our raven spring, beyond those who came
for calving season; for two days, a flock of sixty or more
arrived like a flash mob and patterned the sky. I squinted at
interstices to see what Escher might have seen, maybe white
ravens or fish? I don't know, but I know this, it was unkind
to label flocks of ravens "an unkindness" or a "conspiracy."

I'd like to right this wrong, rename them, an "exuberance,"
or a "fascination," retire those other names so undeserved.
It's true; they have faults, but let's keep in mind the question
about casting the first stone.

MARCH

Four ravens fly over the creek.
Sun glinting off of their backs
they're heading south for now,
who knows what kind of mission
they are on. They are in close
formation, no soaring today,
their strong wings beating, beating,
raven business is calling them,
their shadows trailing along.

March is a busy time for ravens,
bald eagles, and yesterday, a pair
of goldens too. The Black Angus
are birthing; the birds are studies
in patience perched with their backs
to us in trees.

They fill the trees across the creek,
train keen eyes on cattle; they know
when to swoop in and clean up.
They know when to come, and they
know when to go; they have other
appointments to keep.

Watching the Flight School

Swallows covered the rooftop of our garage,
barn swallows and tree swallows. Some lined
the peak; others staged on slanted green metal.
It was a swallow flying school as they hopped
into flight, taking a turn around the garden shed.

Their flights jerky and quick as they learned
how to wheel about and snap bugs from the air
simultaneously. We stepped aside lest they collide
with us in their un-mastered solos, both of us
amazed by this gathering of newly fledged birds.

Even if they were not yet captains of the sky,
seeing their ability to defy bounds of gravity
made my arms and legs feel stone heavy, and
weighted to the ground.

March Day on Beaver Creek

A sound sure as a face cut made by an ax,
the decisive first chop to fell a tree—no ax
needed—a fierce north wind found a punky
spot on a vigil tree by the creek, one of many
burnt reminders of fire along this waterway.

Black cottonwoods burned and boiled, a wonder
they're upright; branches clack and creak in wind.
The noise I heard was so loud it turned my head.
Watching the tree fall I heard a rush of air, saw
water rises like a brief hallelujah in the storm.

One less reminder of the Carlton Complex Fire
is heartening, as is seeing a profusion of tender
saplings among the burnt. The old sentinels may
nurture the new, and certainly they cast their seed.

RECIPROCITY

Daily I startle

California quail,

the whir of their wings

startles me.

I'm sorry I've flushed them.

I'm certain I look

Chaplinesque,

my over-reaction

would play well

in a silent movie.

The quail find another

bush, or tall grass for cover,

or fly to the limb

of a tree and chastise me

with their Woody Woodpecker

like calls that seems as wrong

as a Bald eagle's chortle.

Despite the ludicrous

bird talk, I love seeing quail;

they appear to move

on invisible wheels

rolling quickly along,

their six-feathered plume

leads the way, so peaceful

in their wanderings.

I wish there were words
I could whisper to reassure,
let them know there's no need
for alarm, or maybe

I should wear a hat
with a cocky plume
like hats my Grandmother
wore, or realize racing hearts
might be good for all of us
now and then.

Starlings Return, Early May

Murmurations of starlings
cloud the sky at dusk,
their close formation
beguiles the eye; do they
follow a flight leader?

The whole feathered
cloth of their unison
darkens the sky
in their search
for a roosting place.

To think, it is all because
of Shakespeare's Hotspur
and Eugene Schieffelin
that they're here in the USA.

Iridescent in the right light,
dullish brown when not,
starlings are not loved
by all, but loved by some
for feeding on crane flies,
and if only everyone knew
how they care for their elders,
give them the warmest spots
amid the flock on cold nights.

Would that not endear them
to Hotspur's bird,
unless it said "Mortimer,
Mortimer, Mortimer"
repeatedly?

Covid-19 Days Goldfinches (April 9, 2020)

Goldfinches are back at the feeder,
in bright yellow summer clothes,
our state bird of Washington, free
to migrate, free to congregate, free
of knowing the state we are in with
this pandemic.

We welcome their bright flash
of feathers, their agile beauty
as they sway on a stalk of grass.

One day we'll move freely about again,
congregate, hug family and friends,
and let's pray it's before goldfinches
return to their muted winter plumage.

THE BONUS

We didn't buy this house to fill
a birder's life list, birds are a bonus,
a benefit too, with their symphonic
chirps, tweets, coos, eagle chortles,
and hoots of owls to soothe at night,

Spring brings hummingbirds, a tiny
Calliope, first to our feeder, lets us know
it's time to put it up. Occasionally, four
hummers settle down to drink without
territorial squabbles.

Five vacant birdhouses await tenants.
Wrens put prickly twigs of bayberry
in houses, a surprise to us. The birds
are not dependent on our nesting boxes
or bird feeders; the shrub-steppe provides

what they need, and the creek as well.
We feed in winter and early spring, and
hummers all summer long. These visitors
give us so much enjoyment—our binoculars
often to our eyes.

March Day Find

I found a jawbone,
tiny, but so exact, curved,
with every tooth in place.

After the snow melts,
I am often stooped over,
picking up rocks tossed

by the snowblower
onto the grass; and there
it was a skeletal piece.

A shrew's perhaps.
A reference is needed:
if I trimmed the fingernail

of my ring finger
into a small crescent,
it's that big or that small.

A wonder, beheld
in the palm of my hand.

GONE

The bone-white snag above Beaver Creek fell
in a storm. It was a two-tined fork pointed
skyward, a favored perch of magpies, its alabaster
brightness a cynosure obscured the trees beside it.

It began to lean after heavy spring rains saturated
the ground; we thought it might take down a tree
beside it but instead sheared off only a few limbs.

Now the space it occupied appears gap-toothed,
and gone forever is its sculptural beauty—that fork
tuning the wind—will be missed until memory
of it fades and what is not there is what is there.

SPRING SNOW

Cottonwood trees along Beaver Creek glow.
Backlit by a setting sun, luminous pendants
of seeds hang from limbs, an ornamentation
of progeny, and from each comes a dazzle
of silky haired fluff to swirl in a breeze.

A blizzard begins: seeds go sideways, change
direction and the air is thick with propagation.

Where cottonwoods thrive, female trees
do what's necessary to reproduce—nature's
determination for survival—and afterward,
seeds whiten green lawns, fuzz foundations
and roadsides; masses dance on hard surfaces.
Some seeds can travel miles away.

When the storm finishes, we forget it happened—
being surprised every spring surprises us.

Recast

O earth, your tug and pull:
last night I dreamt I fell,
like quicksilver the spill
of my body, down, down
to the hard, hard, ground,
and my reflexive hand
thrust out like a mother's
to somehow catch myself.
Inside the wrist, bones
take the impact badly:
shatter   split   stab.
Body rises slowly to sit,
startled, by disturbance
of a pleasant walk.
This dream a nightmare,
this re-enactment—
a slip on an icy surface.
Gravity—I know full well,
my hips and other bones
know—you are there,
patiently waiting.

Requiem

Lungs of the March lion breathe heavily, such exhalations in its roar,
raindrops held by its force on windowpanes, blow-down of trees.

One large old cottonwood came down and blocked our roadway,
sliced through an elderberry, where only last year I admired clusters
of berries within easy reach, as limbs arched over the split rail fence.

The shrub made shade, refuge for birds, now a pile of woody debris
instead of new growth, thoughts of picking berries this year, dashed,
thoughts of pausing in admiration, gone.

Before Snowmelt in the Methow

Tight knots of buds tip the ends of limbs,
and beneath the ground, sprouts spear out
of bulbs. Dogs dig in snow, following a scent
of voles busy below. People still enjoy winter
sports: snowboarding, trekking on snowshoes,
they downhill, heli-ski, and cross country ski.

Gardeners turn to other pursuits, tearing open
seed packets to start flowers, herbs or vegetables
in little pots on windowsills, and busily sharpen
their tools. Winter's whiteness having lost its allure,
they look out their windows with impatience.

Spring readies itself in gardeners' bodies, coiled
taut inside, eagerness to smell and feel the soil,
a keen desire for their own unfurling.

*—Gardeners in the Methow wait until the last patch of snow
melts off a nearby mountain: for me it is McClure.*

Every spring, we see a family of marmots
in a shed off Highway 20; to us, they mean
spring is here when they sun on the rooftop
or look out the window. "Marmie," we yell
in delight. We think how cool they'd look
wearing sunglasses and shorts, a cool drink
in hand with a little umbrella embellishment.
Even without, they are one of those constants
we look for, like arrowleaf, or hummingbirds;
they mark the seasons and give us continuity.

The Spring Caller

came one day, the marmot did,
stood on the bank in our backyard,
sun glinting off his golden chest
like highlights on his fur.

He surveyed our house, maybe us too;
we watched amazed by his presence,
the famous or infamous whistle pig,
not loved by homeowners who don't
want them in crawlspaces or sheds.

We enjoyed his visit; lucky for us
he moved on, not to be seen again.
Maybe he found a better place to live
and nibble grass, a better place to burrow,
a place without a dog.

RECONCILIATION

After the snowmelt, when oozy mud dries
and turns to dust, everything is dull, lifeless,
and brown. Stunned by this bleakness, I miss
the thick ermine coat hiding what lies beneath
until greening begins. Sprouts come up quickly.
You could feel them growing if you had time.

Suddenly trees have leaves, plants flourish,
hills shout springtime bedecked with balsamroot,
speckled with it in clutches where dropped seed
found conditions prime, and tiny purple flowers
en masse shade the curvature of hills.

Enraptured by spring's finery, bemoaning our drab
world gives way to stowing away winter garments,
opening windows to air out the house. We'll enjoy
the flowering of trees and shrubs, and settle in
for a new season as we watch species of birds return
from faraway places, and I'll make my peace with
this change, and relegate my snowshoes to a shelf.

Watching and Waiting

—Inspired by Edna St. Vincent Millay's last line in "Spring:"
"Comes like an idiot, babbling and strewing flowers."

A kite-flying wind is steady this last day of March; we watch

last season's crisp Norway maple leaves tumble and scurry

across the lawn like small critters. New leaves, pistachio green,

will soon burst forth, eventually turning a rich burgundy, restful

for eyes on bright summer days.

At this winter-spring transition, red-winged blackbirds greedily

empty feeders until other sustenance is found, wind stirs and stirs

with nature's busyness. Hills will soon green up, be covered

in golden balsamroot and purple lupine, a riot of color to see

on the shrub-steppe.

At this juncture, we'll gladly take babbling and flowers, even this

wind; we've slogged through mud season, and we are ravenous

for spring and a release from winter's grip.

BALKY HILL CATTLE RANCH

Sunday morning
an entire herd
across the creek
lying down
as if they know
it's a day of rest.

Worship for them:
sound of a tractor
lick of salt
sip of water
friends to nuzzle
calves to nurture.

Another day
cows are sorted
some loaded into
a livestock carrier
a bovine opera
begins: keening
of unrest, despair,
and separation.

On another day
watch them form
a line
follow one another
single file
and I wonder

how they choose
their leaders
and follow them
so willingly?

AFTER THE FIRE

Beaver Creek was a river this spring, wild, wide,
and roiling. Our generous snowpack melted quickly
off hillsides without vegetation to bank water—runoff
surged—roots of burnt Ponderosa pine and Doug fir
were impotent as well.

The surge brought silt, pushed snags, tumbled boulders
along. The creek bed, diverted for the sake of salmon, failed;
water sought its old straight course with a vengeance, alongside
the Beaver Creek Road beyond Balky Hill Road, undercut it
both sides, and washed out pavement in its flood.

First, fire ravaged, then water. Now the creek is again within
man made margins; it burbles gently, but its free rein gallop gave
frogs a place to chorus in a new backwater. Mother Nature
once again gave notice of her ways, humbling as she can be.

The Unexpected Guest

A loud and rapid, *whap, whap, whap*, of something hitting our house repeatedly caught my attention. I went to find the source of this sound, and outside the kitchen door, the noisemaker sat, as if he lived here, as if he were waiting for me to call him inside, fill his bowl with Meow Mix, or Friskies Cat Chow. My heart swelled with feline love, "kitty, kitty," I thought, and then noted his size, ears, and white, black, and topaz coat. He turned and looked at me, as I stood polar bear-like in a fuzzy white robe. His eyes widened with a look I interpreted as disgust. He didn't appear to like what he saw, even if I liked what I was seeing. I turned away briefly, called Jack to come downstairs to see him, but kitty was gone.

He was around the neighborhood: the Hoksbergen's dog, Daisy, chased him up into the rafters of their hay shed, and Candy Hoksbergen took a photograph of him.

We saw him cross Upper Beaver close to Highway 20. There were a few more sightings, and then no more, as far as we knew, but I'll always think of him or her and remember the day the bobcat sat on the patio outside the kitchen. I never figured out what the bobcat might have been after, that it had penned there swatting at it against the house, a bird or a mouse maybe, but I'm glad it did so alerting me to its being there.

COVID-19 Days and Killdeer

Killdeer are back. I walk across stubble
in the alfalfa field, startle a pair that flushes
to my left that loudly calls their name.
They take flight, instead of their broken
wing ruse, with zigzag staggering to lead
me away from their nest.

Still, I was led to thoughts of the ocean:
wet sand, a roar of breaking waves, a walk
from Arch Cape to Hug Point in Oregon.
How soothing it would be to be there, to see
plovers run along the tideline, but if we must

shelter in place, this is the place to be, at home.
We'll watch birds nest this ominous spring, see
their young fledge, and how life in nature goes
on undisturbed by this pandemic. I'll be careful
to watch my steps in the fields, looking out for
a scrape of nest with mottled eggs.

Disregarding the Tenth

Arrowleaf balsamroot grows
on my neighbor's property,
and in profusion across the road,
covering hillsides, but here—none.

Humans stripped this land bare
to grow potatoes, later to raise
fallow deer, then alfalfa, and finally,
turf rolled out for a perfect lawn.

Chances seem to be low for seeds
transported by birds or wind to start
arrowleaf balsamroot growing here.
Maybe I should buy seed, cast it, and wait
to see if it germinates, wait three years
more for its bloom, knowing all the while
my eyes are free to trespass and covet
my neighbor's gold.

TRANSFORMATIONS

Either side of the path
to the compost pile,
white serviceberry petals
filtered down,
littered the ground,
looked like long grain rice.

Showered by them, momentarily,
I felt like a bride,
I could almost feel my veil
and blushing expectations,
my head slightly bowed.
What a sensation

A smile formed on my lips
as I carried a vessel,
a cylindrical bouquet
of orange, banana, and apple
peels to toss atop a pile,
a transformation for me

in my imagination, a fruitful
transformation for trees
first bedecked with flowers,
later with sweet purple berries.

SPRINGTIME BLESSINGS

The first wild rose shows its face
to the sun and wind, and me.
So many wild roses on this place,
I am grateful for this bounty,
its beauty, the blessing of sight,
and, a sense of smell which soon
will enjoy another scent, another
reason to revel in springtime,
even though I mourn each change
of season, thinking this is the one
I love best; this is one I wish lasted.

Then a reckoning—an acceptance—
knowing I will love the garnet rosehips
when formed, when frosted with ice,
finally, too, thorny brambles, withstanding
winter to leaf out in spring, and if lucky,
once more, I will greet the first wild rose.

OBSERVATION

Two bulls push each other head-to-head
in Troy's field, a battle for dominance?
They pivot thirty, sixty, ninety degrees,
then they cha-cha forward and back,
forward and back.

An older, bigger bull watches, grunts,
but the dance goes on. It could be play,
exercise, or a way to pass their time,
and maybe it strengthens them, teaches
bullish lessons. I watch only a while.

I have my own dance steps to follow; a list
nudges me along, although it feels as if I
also pivot, sometimes go in circles, and there
is resistance of my own making, and lessons
I need to learn time and time again.

Spectrum (ROYGBIV)

Here, rainbows create one true arc, the ends pocketed
in folds of hills across from us. Our buckets could
overflow with gold if we wanted to fill them.

We've allowed the popsicle-rich colors to sweeten our day,
happy there was rain that came before it, and to live
in wide-open land with room for resplendent shows.

Just as rain soaks into the soil, all those colors soak into
our souls, and so we stand and take rainbow baths in cobalt
and iris, parsley, and peach; allowing the entire spectrum
to wash through us.

SUMMER

Looking Out

Either side of Beaver Creek, cumulus clouds
create a play of light on hills; shadows give
depth to drainages—mother earth in repose—
contours sensuous and unabashed: shoulders,
breasts, hips, thighs.

Hilltops stand out markedly, overlap from afar
as silhouettes; only the tallest sketch the horizon.
To the east, Coyote Ridge hides the sun or moon's
rising as golden or rosy light limns the crest line.

When sun is low in the sky, and mist rolls in,
the world is ethereal; a wistful chiffon curtain
softens everything; other times, clouds with grey
bellies of rain pass us by, or dangle scarves of virga,
to tease us as it evaporates.

Transformations by weather and light change
views minute-by-minute; every morning I sip
my tea, waiting to see what unfolds. Some days,
it's a spectacular full arch of rainbow from
Pole Pick to Wolf Canyon, so close we could walk
in the vibrancy of it, but, instead, we stand in awe.

AFTERWARDS

Ravens are tractor wise; they notice
fields being cut, know little critters
will scurry, having lost cover; ravens
notify kin that the hunt is on: They will
skim above a freshly mown field, land
to stalk through it, picnic in the field
or fly away with take out.

It's all about food: the mown alfalfa
will become big round bales, trucked
away to feed cattle through the winter;
those cattle will be feed for some people.
What am I in this mix beyond consumer,
carnivore, herbivore? Tibetans have it
right—a sky burial, once our soul flies away.

REALIZATION

As I walk our property
a daily round, the dog with me,
his walk or my walk, your guess
as good as mine; I think of all
the life I crush beneath
my feet, a giant invading
other worlds.

I know when I scale the knoll,
stand atop it where pine straw
crosshatches the soil, and carpets
it, the sage I've brushed by
and also trod upon releases
a scent like exotic incense,
my feet a pestle to earth's mortar
to bring that essence into the air.

Blue Mysteries

Flitting from stem to stem in the alfalfa field,
blue moths or butterflies look like flowers
metamorphosed, given wings and freedom,
unleashed from stems where movements
required a breeze. I watch them flutter from
petal to petal, landing momentarily.

They always fly low as if assigned an altitude
by an air traffic controller for their kind.
I'm sure the ecology of diet and egg-laying
dictates this. Perhaps someday I'll learn the name
of these summer visitors, these flowers in flight,
until then I acknowledge them with a lighter heart.

LEARNING TO BE

Not an expert gardener, I enjoy
plants that easily root, and thrive,
give us color, and for nourishment
strawberries satisfy.

I'm never alone; my dog watches me
from a shady spot. I'm entertained
by chirps of birds, shrieks of hawks
and squawks of ravens, and soothed
by the swash of Beaver Creek.

At the family home in Bellingham
I remember my mother on her knees
weeding; as a teenager, I pitied her
for having nothing better to satisfy
her grass widow days.

I didn't know she, in prayerful attitude,
had all that mattered: her home, freedom
to do whatever she chose, and the scent
of God's sweet earth.

HIRUNDO RUSTICA

Early June, swallows investigate sites for nests,
begin to daub mud beneath the eaves of our house;
superstition says not to disturb them; so, we side
with a myth we hope will protect us. We'll witness
open beaks like golden bouquets; to hear a chorus
of their *cheeps*, is one reward.

We keep our luck, clean up droppings, watch babies
fledge, and learn to fly. At sunset, as light slants over
Balky Hill and Beaver Creek, it dazzles in a glitter
of insects. Swallows in aerobatic flight climb, dive,
perform Cuban Eights; beaks snap, *click, click, click*—
like a jazz musician's fingers—as they catch their dinners.

HE WASN'T FERDINAND

Mary Oliver said good morning to wrens,
we said good morning to a large black bull.

He crossed Beaver Creek from a rancher's place.
In open range country, we're responsible to fence
cattle out, not ranchers' to keep them in.
We've moved cows before but not a Black Angus
bull, and he might be cheerful, grazing here.

This is his second day to come here; as he plods
along, large holes form, his hooves sinking deep
into the driveway's shoulder. Other signs the dog
notices; we pray he does not roll in bull perfume.
This is life in Central Washington and thoughts

of a huge black bull wandering in the dark of night
are disturbing. I fear for the corn patch and flowers.
With room to spare, this bull bumped into the rain
gauge, broke supports for new Aspen trees, took out
some fence rails, and, though this isn't a china shop,
I truly wish it were no bull.

WAITING (2018)

A pair of bald eagles were busy in February
on a dead cottonwood tree by Beaver Creek,
remaking an old nest that survived a fire.

I eyed it as I walked our puppy in the snow
on the many outings a puppy needs; he could be
a meal for them to carry away. I kept him close.

At night sometimes I heard their inexplicable
chirpy staccato calls and appreciated their company
in the dark.

They made preparations. We were watchful
of the nesting birds, her white head a marker
of brooding presence and patience.

Her mate sat in another tree close by, and
we were as expectant as they might have
been, and longed to see little eaglet heads

peek above the lip of the large nest, hopeful
we'd also see them fledge. But one day,
the white head visible for months was gone,

her mate as well. Stillness enveloped the nest
and an emptiness that hollows souls.

Our Empty Nest

Once only grey fluff, beak, and eyes
defined him as bird. He was fed—
grew dark feathers, a big hooked beak,
and crazy, outsized, taxicab-yellow feet.
Tended by parents, until only the male
brought food, and rested on a limb
watchful, weary looking, until he left too.

The immature then used the same limb
to occasionally exercise his wings.

His first solo flight was a downward glide
to a leafed tree. We saw him go, later still,
heard him call; we wondered, had he tasted
Beaver Creek? On sweltering days, we'd seen
his beak open, tongue out, looking parched.
We'd watched him daily, through a spotting
scope since he'd hatched. Would he survive,
we wondered? He'd fledged. The great bowl
of sticks crowning the dead cottonwood,
empty, a leafless tree, barren once more.

Watching the Nest (2019)

Feathers fly out of the nest,
not of inhabitants; a bird
is plucked, a California quail
unable to flee, gripped by talons,
taken to an insatiable eaglet.
This eaglet had no mercy for
a smaller sibling, struck it fiercely
with his beak; the little one cowered,
shouldered away when food arrived.
Survival of the fittest is for those
first to the table, hungry and
thirsting for life.

II.
They were just grey fluff at first,
little eaglets; the largest hatched
first; we were glad to see them;
their round, bright eyes gave them
away in the nest of sticks they blended
into, long awaited offspring of two
eagles. The expectant parents took
turns as egg-sitter and nest-protector.
I resisted giving the hatchlings names,
accepted, I could not save the little one.
As one grew, the other diminished, and
one day simply wasn't there.

III.

We watched the survivor. His downy feathers
changed; dark pin feathers appeared, and he
raised his wings now and then, unfolded
and readjusted them, then folded them in
again, a feathered football with head, beak,
and puffy jodhpurs, finished off by ungainly,
gold-yellow feet, which allowed him to move
comically about the nest. Talons aren't made
for walking.

IV.

Fledged: the nest empty. Out of habit, we look
at it, but the young eagle is gone. At first, he took
short flights and returned, until the day he soared
gloriously, wheeled the updrafts, free of the hot sun
on his back, in the leafless tree that held his nest.
We heard he might be flying with a parent down
the creek a ways; when driving, I searched the skies
and treetops hoping to see him. We are happy
he survived, yet he had become part of our day
and lives, and now we must wish him a long
and healthy life.

On the Steppe

Wind blows, and shepherds round balls
cartwheeling everywhere, launches them
high into the sky, ungainly, wingless birds.
They rest atop emerald green alfalfa almost
like big blossoms; seeds drop and are sown;
it's Russian thistle, commonly, tumbleweed,
by any name, it's here, and thrives.

When I was a child in Nevada, older boys
made forts with it, ringed stockades beyond
our housing area where the Mojave spread wide
open and flat. Tumbleweeds roamed like free range
cattle, moving across the land until a shift in wind
brought them back to pile up against any obstacle.

In my Arizona years, people made prickly snowmen
of them, adding a suggestion of carrot nose, smiling
mouths, and dressed them with hats and scarves.
They went well with aluminum trees of the sixties,
and those unlikely dreams of having a white Christmas
 in the Valley of the Sun.

I hate encountering tumbleweeds while driving. I remember
not to swerve, crunching through them. Unlike hitting a deer,
there's little damage, no blood, no carcass to drag roadside,

only a scattering of twigs and seeds, but oh, those seeds, 250,000 per plant, and who wishes to be Johnny or Joanna tumbleweed? They reseed themselves relentlessly, sometimes we help the process, whether we wish to or not.

The Eye of Ra

Trimming lavender, I came face-to-face with a praying mantis.
She turned her green triangular head to me with purple antennae
regal as an Egyptian deity, then slowly turned away to study stem
and leaves for whatever prey would satisfy. In profile, her eye
was as ancient as the Eye of Ra.

I stepped aside with my shears, allowed my partner to photograph her
with his macro lens—then left the mantis to her realm—later we'd marvel
at her image magnified.

Humans named Wonders of the World that can be seen at a distance
instead of minute miracles like a green praying mantis gifted with both
stereoscopic and binocular vision. What wonders she must see. I wonder
what she senses; even with my shears in hand or my partner's camera
focused upon her, she seemed to know we weren't a threat, to her
we might have been mere vassals kneeling in homage.

WITNESS

Fine horizontal silver strands travel above alfalfa fields,

straight as lines on sheets of music or ledgers; they glisten,

underscore clouds in sunlight. One, two, three, I see

one after another, witness each spider's excursion

on the slightest zephyr, cast on silk from spinnerets,

threads robust as steel.

The spiders, too tiny to see, are towed to a new place.

Do they smile; feel a thrill zipping along? I wonder how

they know when to go, impulse, or calculation? What

could we learn from these little Charlottes if we knew

their language, and deigned to listen?

RAINMAKER WANTED

I saw a woman yesterday
in Winthrop, with an umbrella—
not for rain; rain hasn't been
in the forecast, fire has. Fears
and anxieties are kept in check,
but, beneath skin, muscles tense,
jaws tighten.

I saw a woman with an umbrella
sheltering herself from sun. I wish
it had been for rain, not a sprinkle,
but a downpour: a gullywasher,
a drenching rain, a grab everything
left outside soaking rain, one that
washes dust off my car, flattens
tall grass, and makes the earth
smell sweet. I would dance naked
in a rain like that.

August Days

Hills in the Methow are brown and dry.
hollyhock rattles in the wind; seeds drop;
they cover the ground like googly eyes
and stare.

The puppy rescues items from the compost;
everything in the world is a toy, even a large
green tomato, or dried leaf on a stem. He stalks
the strawberry bed hoping to find a berry to eat.

A frog in a tall pot by the front door surprises me.
He's sitting in the shade of rosemary. He must be
a tree frog able to scale the side of the house;
there's no other way he could have gotten there.

No doubt, I'll look for him now when I go in or out.
I'll feel sad when other frog business calls him away.

Smoke rolls in from British Columbia or Oregon.
I feel for people who have lost homes and gardens.
In the Methow, we know about fires and loss,
but also about plants growing back, houses rebuilt,
people finding their way. Disaster saddens us;
yet, what miracles there are, resiliency, frogs
finding shade, hollyhock determined to reseed.

West Side Longings

A small emerald green isle
in the shade of a fence post,
in the upper field where all
is twiggy, straw-colored,
crisp and dry.

What an oasis this small patch
of moss is; tender shoots wave
in the wind; only my eyes travel
this terrain, a Lilliputian paradise,
only my eyes and imagination.

A sweet coolness emanates
from it. I wish to walk barefoot
there, then stretch out, hands
clasped behind my head, and
sleep a deep undisturbed sleep
on the sublime greenness of it.

Fire Season

Flycatchers flit by windows looking
suicidal in their efforts to catch bugs,
as I begin my day sipping tea, I take stock
of the world around me.

Today it is hazy, and I could wish
it were fog, but it's smoke from a fire
up Twisp River growing in acreage,
and people make plans on what to do
with livestock, pets, themselves.

Greyness colors their world and ours.
A large map outside Hank's supermarket
shows the fire's progress each day,
and people stop to talk and walk
away with prayers for firefighters,
with prayers for homeowners,
with prayers for themselves.

Rain in Central Washington

There are days
my west side roots
feel watered by rain,
my soul grateful
for a respite from sun,
even if I love blue skies,
and rotund cumulus clouds.

For me, a grey day is like
a cozy old robe I cinch
around me, a reason
to cocoon, to write,
or read, to be inside,
and I know other roots
are drinking deep, and when
I hear a bird singing
a tremolo, I wonder
if it is a rejoicing for this
day that does not parch?

TRICKSTER DREAMS

The old recurring nightmare was back,
but shifted to something entirely new—
I found myself in a pack of wolves, or maybe
coyotes; some nipped at my heels, and one,
inexplicably, found a way to sit beside me
on the bicycle I was riding. Cheek-to-cheek
I told him about dog food in cans, of kibbles
and table scraps. His eyes showed an interest
in everything I said. He sniffed me. I told him
he was a good dog; I knew he would not harm me.

Morning came with sunlight and birdsong
ending sleep and dreams, a savior from
torments, severing, as well, such astonishments.

SUMMER STORM

For two nights lightning
lit up our world in strobe-light
flashes silver-grey; the world
inside and out appeared
like old photograph negatives.

Thunder made us huddle close,
the two of us and the dog, while
the noise rumbled much too close—
rain hitting the metal roof hard,
drumming, and drumming, and
through a slightly cracked window
an eerie whistle of wind, the same
made the Norway maple
called "crimson sentry" shake
violently—it was a sight to see.

Power failed, electronics beeped,
clocks stopped, and somewhere near
Rainy Pass in the North Cascades
rocks and mud slid over Highway 20
burying it twenty-five feet deep,
stranding some motorists.

After all the meteorological mayhem
the following day dawned clear,
our bird bath was full, a small washout
on the driveway required attention
and a need to windrow the cut alfalfa
was obvious, but for songbirds
all was again right in the world and
they filled the air with sweet sounds.

VISITORS

And so the guests have gone;
thank goodness for that and
the restoration of quiet mornings
without all that chatter and
someone turning on the television
to listen to news, or I should say
ad-libbing through it as if the inanity
of commentators is not enough.

Oh, it is fine to have visitors come,
but finer too to see them go,
and to think my parents called me
the social one. They were wrong
about that, but how I would welcome
them if I could turn back time, watch
their truck and trailer come up
the driveway, have tea with my mother,
offer my dad a cold beer, and ask them
all the questions that now come to mind.

FALL

Three Aspen Trees

—For Luther Allen

Eyes on the boles
of aspen trees
are whimsical,
their leaves as well,
almost heart-shaped.
I stand in the middle
of the three we planted,
feeling some kinship
as I look around
at the landscape;
they see/I see
and listen,
and wonder
how these trees
can imitate
rainfall
so well;
they also whisper
in a breeze.
I strain to hear
what they're saying,
feeling certain
it has something/everything
to do
with peace.

FEAST

Ravens issue the invitation—a raucous one—
throaty voices calling over and over,
their circling flight provides the address;
some sit on fence posts awaiting their turn
but call out—oh, how delectable the feast—
in the deep snow a trail of blood,
evidence of the coyote's last steps
near the base of a hill off Upper Beaver Creek.

Party crashers come: magpies, eagles—
the golden takes his place at the head of the table,
his body ratchets up and down, great beak
tearing flesh—the ravens and magpies nibble
at the periphery, but when the golden eagle
raises a taloned foot or shifts slightly
the smaller birds skitter out of range
of the great bird's talons or beak.

Nearby three bald eagles perch in trees,
a study in patience, they will take their turns—
the splayed body of the coyote diminishes
in size bite-by-bite as the birds feast,
and the remains provide sustenance
to less obvious nocturnal visitors, or insects
and will quietly decompose; but presently
the carcass and blood-splattered snow
is a busy, noisy place of birds big and small,
of hierarchies and appetites.

BEAVER LOVE

At night as I sleep, beavers paddle ashore, find trees
to fell, leave a stump sharpened like a big pencil
stuck in the earth. Such diligence from a creature once
hunted for hats and coats, still trapped for castoreum.

I've lived in places named for things long gone; no buckeyes
on Buckeye Street in Vacaville. On Forest Street, in Bellingham,
our house on the South Hill stood where a once dense forest
covered the entire area; settlers came, cut it all down to ship logs
to San Francisco after the great fire, and lumber mills began.
Streets were named in remembrance of trees that once grew
there: Cedar, Alder, Pine, Maple, and Fir.

Living by Beaver Creek, I'd love to see one beaver paddle along,
webbed hind feet propelling it, tail-rudder at work. To know
they're here is enough, of course, to know some people accept
them now, and that they're relocated to places to reduce erosion,
and bring up the water table, but still, one sighting would please me,
one moment to whisper welcome home.

Last Flight

A loud thunk on a window,
something large hits it. The dog
barks and barks. On the patio,
a kestrel on his back, chest heaving,
talons grasping the last bit of life
 he will know.

His body cradled in my hands,
how I wish a light in his eye
would signal revival; he'd startle,
turn, and fly away.

I say a short eulogy and let him go,
toss his body skyward for one last
flight until gravity takes him down,
down into a ravine where some animal
will find him; he'll go on, in another
form. My hands without his weight
feel such an emptiness.

Traveling in Broad Daylight

—In answer to William Stafford's, "Traveling Through the Dark."

A hurt deer by the side of the road, a doe.
I am not William Stafford there was no cliff
to roll her off of, and as far as I know, no fawn
in her belly. Her body was well off the roadway,
no cars would swerve to avoid her, the pavement
that day, slick with rain.

Signs in the Methow tally the number of deer killed,
the cost of damages to vehicles, and anyone who lives
here has seen blood smeared roads, bloated carcasses
off to the side, and knows the feast they provide
avian scavengers.

This deer sat on her haunches, not a normal position,
her head hanging down, she wretched, coughed up blood.
Someone hit this deer, and left her, maybe they called
the game agents to come and dispatch her, I don't know—
all I know is it wasn't soon enough for me—surprised
by the sight of her sitting there, and witnessing her plight,
now etched in memory.

Maybe there should be a third tally for the anguish of these
sightings, for damages, big or small, to human sensibilities.

OPPORTUNITY

Rooster, you call out mornings when the sun
has barely risen, only a fine seam of light starts
you crowing. Scientists say it's not the light,
it's biological and you, the original alarm clock,
sound your distinctive *er ah er ah ooh* at ninety loud
decibels, puncture my dreams and awaken me.

I'd like to be grateful for your cheerful country
sound, for your diligence in doing what comes
naturally to roosters besides making eggs happen,
you seem to be all about morning and breakfast
time, while for me I find my pillow perfectly
plumped for my sleeping head, my sheets soft,
and a comforter wraps around me like a shroud.

On mornings like that Mr. Rooster an evilness
comes over me with thoughts of a hatchet and a
rolling head; in truth I couldn't do that, your head
is safe, as is your morning crowing and perhaps
you're a gift from my muse, and I should follow
William Stafford's model, get up early, eat toast,
lie on the couch and write my first poem of the day.

QUESTIONS

Outside, it appears
so still—
yet, all day birds
wing through the air.
Do they create
wafts or downdrafts?
Do other birds
or insects feel them?

When we hear
the steady sound
of skin, muscle, bone
and feathers
beating through
air, do we not
feel privileged
to be in a silence
that allows this
experience?

These are gifts:
stillness and silence,
and time to wonder.

NEOLOGISM:

Maybe I should Walden today
wrap myself in simplicity
hone down to what matters
what's necessary, enjoy
a cool glass of water
breathe deep
stretch
sit on my milking stool
cut back the lavender
and pray.

BETWEEN OUR FIELD AND MICHAEL AND LESLIE'S

At the hole in the fence,
the dog pauses.

Nose to the ground,
he tries to discern
who comes and goes
from the neighbor's field
to ours, or ours to theirs.

He pauses for a while
in the middle of our walk.
I keep going; he'll catch up.

Some people put up motion
sensitive cameras for photos
of animals wandering at night
like bright-eyed gray ghosts;

we will not; we'll let it all remain
a mystery; of course, the dog
may know, but he will never tell.

Methow Rocks

Boulders on hillsides show up some days
more than others; some look like sheep
grazing; others appear to be large animals
curled up, resting from lumbering about.
It's all about light, clouds, shadows.

In this once glaciated place, boulders
and rocks are plentiful; when farmers
till a field, rocks, large and small, surface
time and time again; before mechanization
they faced backbreaking work.

No doubt many have cursed the rocks,
even if some find ways to use them
for walls, foundations, fireplaces.
One thing is certain; there is no shortage
of them here, nor will there ever be.

GUS AND THE COYOTE

Twice our dog chased a young coyote
who hunts a newly mown field.
Does Gus think he's found a playmate?

Young coyote could be a trickster sent
to lure Gus to a waiting pack who'd pursue
him, making him run and run until his tongue
lolled long and thirsty, his loping gait slowed
and faltered, then they'd circle to attack.

At least that's what I've been told. I'm watchful.
Gus enjoys his freedom to be a canine of the wild,
eyes sparkling, or nose to the ground or wind, aware
of the marvels of the world around him.

Our *Canis familiaris*, like *Canis latrans*, finds so much:
a smorgasbord in grasses, gophers, voles, and mice.
Kibbles and dog biscuits become a bland attempt
to satisfy when his senses alert him to hunt and savor
old family recipes.

Cooper's Concern (2016)

Our neighbor has a brush pile burning.
Tall flames gyrate as fire gobbles oxygen.
Our dog spies this anomaly in territory
he views as his, barks sharp warning
sounds and emits a series of low growls
before he shoots us looks of concern.

We tell him he's a good dog but ask him
to stop, letting him know we know, yet we
wonder does he remember the night we
nervously watched advancing flames
from the Cougar Flat fire which merged
with the Carlton Complex fire of 2014?

Does he remember tension-filled moments
of our evacuation, recall breathing smoke
that hung in the air for weeks afterwards
which the sun could barely burn through?

The dog walks to windows east and west,
surveys all views then lies down with an uneasy,
wary look in his eyes before he makes a few
muffled growls at this most unwelcome intrusion.

REPOSITORY

Walking to the mailbox, I stretch my legs,
look at sky, hear birds sing, and see what's
growing—right now it's tumble mustard—
tall, with golden blooms outlining the alfalfa,
a highlighter of sorts, a weed, like many plants,
growing whether we want them to or not.

I go to check for what I think of as real mail
—in these days of electronic correspondence—
usually only bills or advertisements. When I find
 a letter, carrying it to the house gives my hands
a sense of purpose.

As for junk mail, like weeds, difficult to be free of.
I notify advertisers I don't want to hear from them,
but they are fervent in their attempts to woo me.

Ah, that there were more letter writers to take up
their pens and turn my head with words, to give
my mailbox *raison d'être*, make it a repository of desire
and meaningful dialogue. Someday, I wish to walk
to the mailbox and see it pulse wildly, holding more
letters from friends and relatives than junk mail,
my mailbox revitalized, letter writing back in style.
Well, at least on my walks to it, surveying my world,
I can dream.

Sometime in November

Incrementally, winter arrives; temperatures drop;
we begin adding layers of clothing; notch-by-notch
the thermostat is raised. When the first flakes of snow
waft down, we speculate whether it will stick.

Real change comes when Cascade peaks whiten,
when snow covers ground, a sense of satisfaction
arrives; summer's work is done; dormancy can come.
A feeling of settling in occurs.

For some, anticipation of that whiteness signals surrender:
they close up their houses, pack their bags, head south
to California, Arizona, New Mexico, anyplace warm,
anyplace but the Methow Valley in wintertime.

For those of us who stay, we don't hibernate, but it changes
our routines, changes us; boots become standard footwear
whenever we venture out. The North Cascades Highway
closes, and there's a feeling of being sequestered.

Tourists and second homeowners come to cross-country
ski on the miles of trails, but weekdays, this place has only
locals doing errands, meeting for coffee, mindful of ice.
We carry our slippers when visiting friends.

MY NOVEMBER DAY

—Inspired by Helen Hunt Jackson's first line in "November."
This is the treacherous month when autumn days
begin chilly and crisp, warm midday, and then cool
again. Daylight shortens, and darkness closes in.

I'll feel the loss of summer's lengthened days.
Today, I'll uproot petunias, geraniums, begonias,
and all the flowers planted on a sunny day in spring

to fill whiskey barrels, eight in all, watered daily,
fertilized weekly. The starts became bedraggled
with June's incessant rain, mud-splattered ugly.

I didn't think they'd make it, but in no time, they filled
the planters cascading in a showy profusion of colors.
Butterflies kissed the blooms, while hummingbirds'

tongues probed, and bees disappeared completely
into petals as they gathered pollen. But today is a day
I am murderous in my garden, gloved hands, and tools

ready to uproot these colors and frills. It's frost that kills,
not me, or the sugarcoated look of ice crystals; the freeze
is intercellular taking its deathly toll. Plants wilt and die.

So off I go, a wheelbarrow full of summer to the compost pile.
Winter days are coming when my whisky barrels fill with snow.

MORNING ON BEAVER CREEK

Twenty-two Canada geese in a ragtag line
fill a brief interlude, honking calls, familiar
to the ear, conjure a sense of longing.

My eyes follow their flight and hearkening
sounds until the sky clears of this beckoning,
I am left both enriched and diminished.

Whenever I hear them, a piece of my soul ascends,
falls into their slipstream, and flies away.

Tell Me, William?

—In Answer to William Stafford's, "Ask Me."

Was it springtime when you came to the Methow, rivers surging
beyond banks, swamping aspen, cottonwood, and cinnamon bark
pine? Viewing the valley with forest rangers could you hear them
over the roar of tumultuous rivers well fed by snowmelt?

You saw jagged mountain peaks, to successive rounded hilltops
that shoulder this valley, sought images from Washington Pass
in the Cascades, to the mighty Columbia at Pateros, visited all
the rivers that merge, one into another, all along the way.

Did seeing the Methow in just one season, one visit, constrain
your musings like the Columbia River with miles of its banks
walled by cement, controlled by dams, unable to meander?

You wrote of a frozen river, where you'd be open to questions
about your life, differences made by mistakes or people's love
or hate. Would you have returned in winter if you had lived?

When the Methow River ices over, I'll go to it bundled up
to keep warm. I'll hold on to to winter's stillness and silence.
I'll ask the questions you have posed, and listen to whispered
eddies and wash in the hidden current.

You won't be there to witness sculptural forms of ice along
the banks, or the frozen slate blue river. My breath will fog the air
as I ask your questions. Your poem will be there etched on a sign;
I'll place my notebook by it to jot down what the river says.

Rivers, Creeks and Roads

Arteries of Washington State are the mighty Columbia
which bisects it, while Interstate 5 runs north to south,
and Interstate 90 east to west. The veins are eighty-one
rivers with melodious names: Ozette, Klickitat, Methow,
Nisqually, Cedar, Chehalis, Skagit, Duwamish—to name
only a few, and the creeks, who could count them all?
in the Methow there are so many I'm always astounded.

I live on Upper Beaver Creek. My town and river share
the same name, Twisp. Wherever we go, there's poetry
in place names. Traveling from Bellingham to Twisp,
road signs, for towns I drive past, are familiar and
comforting; like a prayer bead, I grasp and let go of,
moving on to the next: Sedro Woolley, Lyman, Concrete,
Marblemount, Newhalem, Mazama, Winthrop, then
Twisp, and on to a universal place name in our hearts—
home.

ACKNOWLEDGMENTS

With deep appreciation to Mary Gillilan and Norman Green for their support of my writing: Mary, as my editor, and Norman, for the fine printing and binding work of Threshold Documents in Bellingham, Washington. Thanks also, to my dear friends, Mark Reece and Jane Hill for their careful reading of the book, and my writing groups: Mary Gillilan's, Independent Writers' Studio in Bellingham, and Confluence Poets in the Methow Valley. Jack Kienast photographed the red bench where I have a view of the creek. Kathy Brackett provided sketches for chapter headings, and I appreciate her illustrations and talent. I also feel fortunate to have my partner, Jack Kienast's listening ear, and his photographic work and design for the cover and back cover of this book. Special thanks to Jennifer Molesworth, an Upper Beaver Creek neighbor, for her curated exhibit at Confluence Gallery of artists of Upper and Lower Beaver Creek for inspiring this work.

"The Call," *Methow Arts Magazine*, Winter 2017.18. and Confluence Poet's Methow Valley Postcard Series, 2019.

"Cooper's Concern," *Resting in the Familiar*, 2017.

"Covid-19 Days March 24, 2020," Pandemic Poetry Podium, 2020, pandemicpodium.wordpress.com—A virtual gathering for poetry in the time of Covid-19.

"Covid-19 Days April 9, 2020," Pandemic Poetry Podium, 2020, pandemicpodium.wordpress.com—A virtual gathering for poetry in the time of Covid-19.

"The Feast," *Clover, A Literary Rag*, Vol. 5, Summer 2013 and Resting in the Familiar, 2017.

"Life Cycles in the Methow," *Clover, A Literary Rag*, Vol. 8, Winter 2014, and Resting in the Familiar, 2017.

"March Day on Beaver Creek," *Windfall: A Journal of Poetry of Place*, Spring 2020.

"Methow Weather Report," *Resting in the Familiar*, 2017.

"Morning on Beaver Creek," *Resting in the Familiar*, 2017.

"Pine Trees: Two Views," *Clover, A Literary Rag*, Vol. 6, Winter 2013, and *Resting in the Familiar*, 2017.

"Recast," The Shrub-Steppe Poetry Journal, Spring, 2020

"Snowplow Sidewalks," *Clover, A Literary Rag*, Vol. 12, Winter 2016 and *Resting in the Familiar*, 2017.

"Summer Storm," *Windfall: A Journal of Poetry of Place*, Spring 2014, and Resting in the Familiar 2017.

"Visitors," *56 Days of August Poetry Postcards*, 2017.

"Waiting," *Resting in the Familiar*, 2017.

"Witness," *Washington Poetic Routes*. A digital poetry-mapping project by Washington State Poet Laureate, Claudia Castro Luna c. 2019, #52.

"What's Left," *The Shrub-Steppe Poetry Journal*, Spring, 2019.

About At Home on Upper Beaver Creek

In *At Home on Upper Beaver Creek,* Christine Kendall shares her wonderment at the cycle of the seasons. From her home in Central Washington—a landscape of ancient glacier-scraped, boulder-strewn hillsides, forests, and fiercely nourished homesteads—she shows us the "hierarchies and appetites" of eagles and ravens, of torrential rain and fire.

—J.I. Kleinberg, co-editor, *Noisy Water: Poetry from Whatcom County, Washington*

At Home on Upper Beaver Creek, begins with the scree of a red-tailed hawk, a call "like bells ringing the Angelus for prayers, / a singing bowl or gong for meditation calling us to pause." . . . In "Covid-19 Days and Killdeer," she writes, "if we must / shelter in place, this is the place." This book of poems, too, is a sturdy shelter, inviting us in, urging us to make ourselves at home.

—Bethany Reid, author of *Sparrow* and *Body My House*

www.ingramcontent.com/pod-product-compliance
Lightning Source LLC
Chambersburg PA
CBHW040931030426
42334CB00007B/115